CW01433175

THE

RHINO

MENTALITY

THE

RHINO

MENTALITY

Achieve Unstoppable Success

JEFFREY J. DELGADO

The RHINO Mentality: Achieve Unstoppable Success
Copyright © 2017 by Jeffrey J. Delgado
All rights reserved. This book or any portion thereof may not be reproduced or used in any manner whatsoever without the express written permission of the publisher.
Printed in the United States of America.
ISBN-13: 9781546651246
ISBN-10: 1546651241
Library of Congress Control Number: 2017911960
CreateSpace Independent Publishing Platform
North Charleston, South Carolina
Editor: Rick Chavez
Publisher: Chavez Media

Contents

Dedication

To my daughter Shirley, you are truly what drives me everyday!
I am so proud of the beautiful person you have become. I
thank the Lord everyday for blessing me with such an amazing
daughter. I love you more than you will ever imagine!
To my amazing wife and best friend, Emily, thank you for
your never-ending support and being the rock of our family.
You have always been such a true example of love and
beauty, inside and out. Thank you for always believing in
me, Baby! I love you today, but not as much as tomorrow.
To Juju, thank you for always being honest, straightforward
and committed. You are growing into a strong young teen.
Always remember that "mommy's friend" loves you always!
In loving memory of my parents Shirley & Rogelio Delgado.
Special Thanks to David, Josie and Gabriela Pascua, Anthony
(Tuffy), Jonathan, Jennifer, Robert & Kristina Pallen, Carlos
Quintero, Mark & Cyril Senores and my cousin Roger (Rog).

Foreword

I want to discuss the concept of Interested vs. Committed. I've always been interested in playing the piano. My grandpa used to teach piano and many of my cousins learned how to play by taking lessons from him. As time went on, I watched some of my family members play the piano so well and I was amazed by how much they had learned. But, while I've always been interested in learning how to play, I never actually committed myself to doing it.

There is a huge difference between being interested in something and being committed to something. Interested means, "I wouldn't mind doing that." But committed means, "I'm going to make time to make it happen." You find a way when you're committed and you never let anything stop you.

Let's say you want to get in great shape. The first question is, are you "interested" in getting in shape or are you "committed" to getting in shape? Are you "interested" in having a great marriage or are you "committed" to having a great marriage? Interest is for the common person. Most people are interested in a lot of things but they're not committed enough to want to do them.

Through the writing of this book, I will try my best to encourage you to become committed to the life you've always dreamed of.

I've got a friend named Les Schlais who is a legend in the insurance industry. He and I are working on the launch of a blockbuster company that will energize the financial services industry, create incredibly successful solopreneurs and help thousands, if not millions, of people around the United States retire with the security that their hard-earned wealth will be preserved. This is the message Les wanted me to pass along to you.

"I have been in the insurance business longer than I can remember and have started many companies. I've worked with all of the big names in the industry and have seen many of them retire with more than enough. But I've also seen the opposite side of the coin: companies that failed because of poor management or agents who were left out in the cold while the top echelon broke the bank. Worse than all that, I've seen countless hard working Americans lose their life savings due to poor financial planning or the lack of a good insurance policy. It breaks my heart to know that these people trusted our industry and were failed by it.

When Jeff told me that he was going to write this book about The Rhino Mentality, my ears perked up. I know how tough a rhino can be and I admire the characteristics that make it such a formidable animal. If Jeff can train how to have a rhino's thick skin and unrelenting drive, I'm all for it. Jeff has shown me that he has those qualities himself and I've trusted him to train many of my agents in the past, which is why I asked him to join me in launching and building Retiring America.

I have no doubt that this book will be a valuable tool for anyone who has the drive to start their own venture, who wants to advance to a higher level within their current company or just would like to improve their daily habits for living a memorable life. The lessons Jeff teaches will be valuable for anyone at any stage of their lives and career.

Once you're done, please let Jeff know how much you loved his book. I wish you the best in everything you do."

Les Schlais
Founder & CEO, Retiring America

Life is Short

Death is not usually a topic that writers include in a book that is meant to inspire and move others to take action. But I believe the subject of death should be addressed in order to truly understand and appreciate the value of life. Many people are completely scared of death because it represents the unknown. None of us know what it looks or feels like but, because of my belief in God, I have faith that there is a heaven. Based on those Christian faith principles I know what the Bible says about what will happen to me after I die.

I also believe that, before our time is at hand and we leave this world, we should endeavor to live life to the fullest.

DEATH IS REAL

My mother passed away when she was 44 years old and my father died at the age of 68. In a natural sense, I was always pretty sure that I would outlive my parents but God wanted to get them home even earlier than expected. Losing the two of them at such a young age gave me a lot of time to think about my own life and develop a completely different perspective on what I would do going forward. I learned at a young age that life is short and you're not guaranteed tomorrow. You're not even guaranteed that you'll be here in the next twenty minutes. You're not guaranteed that you'll make it out the door today. So, when you find yourself taking life for granted and believing that everything is a routine, you should quickly remember that you've never been in this day of your life. This day has never happened to you or anyone else. These 24 hours have never happened in history and tomorrow will be another day that the world has never seen.

When my kids leave I tell them, "I love you, sweetheart." Because maybe it's the last time I see her. The last words I told my mom were I love you. My brothers were fighting and she told me to tell them to stop. I said I had to go to school and she said, "Bye, honey. I love you." That was the last thing she ever said to me. When she died, my dad asked if I wanted to go to the hospital but I didn't want to see her not alive. It stuck to me. Now I tell my wife and my kids all the time, I love you sweetheart. I text them, I love you. Maybe it's the last time I'm going to say it. So my message is, don't take life for granted.

HOW MANY DAYS LEFT?

I'm in the life insurance business and the studies we use to calculate costs show that the life expectancy in the United States is about 80 years with women living longer, on average, than men. I'm 47 years old as I write this book, which gives me about 33 years to live if you look at an average life expectancy. That means

I have about 33 Christmases, 33 Super Bowls, 33 NBA champion-ships and 33 more birthdays to celebrate. I have a 19-year old daughter named Shirley and by that time she'll be 52 years old. So if I live past her 52nd birthday those would be "extra" years for me. Looking at it this way gives me a different perspective because I view death as how much time I have left on this earth. I know it sounds a little bit morbid but it's something I don't run away from. Most people ignore death completely because it's something in the future, so far from now they can't concern themselves with it. But others, like me, embrace the concept and capitalize on how valuable life really is.

Don't take your life for granted. Don't even take a day for granted. Enjoy every day as much as you can. Ask yourself, how can I be my ab-solute best at what I do? If you're going to be here doing something, be the best at it. If you're going to be in a business, do your best. If you're going to play an instrument, do your best. With anything you do, do your best. Don't take life for granted and go after the things you've always dreamed about. You're only going to be your current age once so go for it.

Because we can easily rewind and replay videos, music or mov-ies from long ago, we have this sense that we can always go back in time. That may work with old film festivals or watching one hit wonders at the county fair but, in reality, you'll never get this time back again. You'll never get back the time it took to read this sentence. Once it's gone, it's gone. You either wasted a moment or embraced a moment. Do your best to embrace every day by finding your gifts. Some of you find your gift when you're young. Some will find it years later. But if you never look for something, you'll never find it. You may get lucky and stumble across one of your gifts but, chances are, you possess many gifts that this world needs to have.

Many people spend their time watching or listening to negative news about war or the economy or diseases. I've heard people say they don't want to have children in this world but I'd like to challenge that thinking. I believe we need more great people who can raise great children. We need more great leaders to be born so that we can be the light in darkness, if you will. I'm not fearful of kids being born into this world because we need more positive impact from them and positive influences from the things they accomplish.

WATCH AND OBSERVE

Some people move so fast they don't even know what's going on around them or what's happening in life. They overlook so many beautiful things. I've seen people go to the best restaurants or hotels in the world, to exclusive sporting events or on fabulous historical tours. But the whole time they're stressing about something else. They're never really present in the moment. They may be in position to have a great time with their kids but they're worried about work. Or they're on a romantic cruise with their spouse but they're preoccupied with financial matters instead.

Observing and being present is one of the areas of my life that I really had to improve on. I found myself thinking so much that I frequently wound up engaging my mind somewhere else. I think it's important that you be present wherever you find yourself. I invite you to go through a day observing life and watching what's happening around you.

I think leaving a legacy is very important to think about. I don't mean your financial legacy; I mean the way you're going to be remembered when you leave this life. What types of memories will you leave behind? How do you want to be remembered by your family and others around you? Will it be as a husband or wife who was loving or as a friend who was always in good spirits with a word of encouragement? Many don't even know what their reflection gives off because they're so used to speaking from the inside. They never notice what everybody else sees from the outside. Try to see yourself from the outside and, if you don't like what you see, adjust your attitude and stop taking your days for granted.

Let's say you found out from the doctor that this was going to be your last year. How would you want it to play out? What would you want to do? What kinds of things would you like to see? What kind of attitude would you have? The moral of this story is to treat every day as if it's your last because one day it will be.

SMILE MORE, WORRY LESS

Without a doubt, you can truly control emotions and how you feel at any moment. For example, when I had a regular job, I always looked forward to Fridays. When the clock hit 5:00pm, I couldn't wait to get out the door so that I could feel free again. I knew I'd be free all day Saturday. I knew I'd be free at church and with family on Sunday. But then the dreaded Monday would arrive. I hated

Mondays so I began to stress and feel more pressure. I started wondering if I had conditioned myself to hate certain days of the week. The answer was a resounding Yes.

I know now that you're supposed to enjoy every single day, understanding that you can't control certain things so you shouldn't stress about them. Sometimes it's a lesson in progress. Losing my mother and my father, in addition to young friends, uncles, aunties and cousins who I loved, put life into perspective. Life is short and it's never as bad as it seems. Life will always put you through a series of trials but you were built to handle them. You just need to have faith that this is merely a lesson that you're going through and you'll make it. Always have a positive outlook in any situation. Smile more and convince yourself that you're always happy. You can control and fool your brain. Exercise your body or take a long run up the hills to help trigger emotional change. It's a proven fact that it's almost impossible to cry while you're jogging so try to keep yourself on the move.

MEMORIES & EXPERIENCES
When you lose your mother at a young age, you often think about the things she missed in life. My Mom didn't get a chance to see her sons get married or play with her grandchildren. That's when I remind myself that life is not about the things you accumulate. It's about the experiences that you take with you. When you're stretched out on your death bed, are you really going to think about the cars and houses you bought or are you going to think about all the moments you've enjoyed with your spouse and

children? Did I do the things that I wanted to do? Did I give love to the people I wanted to give love to?

When you compare a life of accumulation vs. a life of experiences, I vote overwhelmingly for experiences and memories. I know a lot of people like to show off the things they've bought and in this social media world it's all about impressing others but you shouldn't live for that reason. Don't worry about what other people have or what they don't have. I look at it as life fulfillment vs. hoarding material things. Life fulfillment could mean simple things that don't even cost a dime. Like taking walks in the park or running with your dog on the beach, having a great conversation with your spouse over coffee, having breakfast on a regular Tuesday or waking up in the morning when it's sunny (or rainy) outside. Enjoy and treasure every experience.

See more of the things you've wanted to see, go to places you've never been before. Try new restaurants and just enjoy being present. Most people get so busy making a living and paying bills and taking care of their responsibilities that they forget that life is a journey of memories and experiences. It doesn't need to be as difficult as we try to make it. Obviously you need to make a living, I truly understand that. But as you're doing what you have to do to put food on the table and a roof over your head and clothes on your back, please don't forget to have fulfillment in the process. Don't forget to live in the Now. Don't forget to see who and what is really in front of you. Don't be in the middle of a great life and not see it. Life will go by too fast if you're not cherishing it and grabbing on to the memories that are right in front of you.

DO WHAT YOU LOVE

Some people are lucky enough to have once-in-a-generation gifts that others will flock to pay for, like a singer who gets the right break and records a platinum album. Or the author who writes a New York Times best seller and is now in demand for speaking engagements all around the country. Or maybe their gift was in sports and they made it to the highest professional level and the Hall of Fame. Although there are many who are born with those special gifts, most of us are content with the more humble gifts we were blessed with.

As you pursue your dreams, do what you love, chase what you love, love your life, love the fact you have a job and appreciate that you're healthy enough to work. But don't mistake income for passion. I talk to many people who hate their jobs and wish they could switch but the job may actually be getting them closer to their passion than they know. Be looking for your passion and gifting in all situations. If your life becomes the same week after week after week, you could miss out on your gifts because you became a routine yourself. You need to be growing on a daily basis. Learn how to love to learn. You can learn from every single person you meet and from every book you read. Sometimes I like to watch movies or read books that can teach me a lesson. Be a student of learning so that you're constantly growing and challenging your mind. Don't believe that your mind has enough information already. You can always bring more to that wonderful brain.

The sales world can be tough because you think you need to act a certain way to attract business. But attempting to impress or please everyone is probably the worst thing you can do. Quit worrying about what other people think. Do what you believe is right.

If you're ever confused, continue to do what's right. Follow your passions and do everything with love and you'll enjoy a much more fulfilling life journey.

Ordinary vs. Altered State

Most people live their day-to-day lives in what I call the "ordinary state of consciousness." I define the ordinary state of consciousness as the way we normally operate throughout our lives. The ordinary state is just that, ordinary. You do certain things the same way every day and everything works the way it's supposed to work, everything is good and you're satisfied with the results you're getting. My belief is that, while you may think that everything is fine in your ordinary state of consciousness, you can rise up to an even greater, more fulfilling level.

Most people are probably not tapping into this higher level and that's a shame. Instead of being comfortable in your ordinary state of consciousness, I would encourage you to move to an "altered state of consciousness" and live what I call the authentic life. It's authentic because you're living the life that you envisioned long ago in your dreams while living with more creativity, energy and excitement. Do you remember when you were in high school and how excited you were to go out with your friends at the end of the week? It was so cool and yo u couldn't wait to scream, "Thank God It's Friday!"

The goal of an authentic life is to make every ones of your days a Friday because that's when you're living out your dreams and when you become the highest version of yourself.

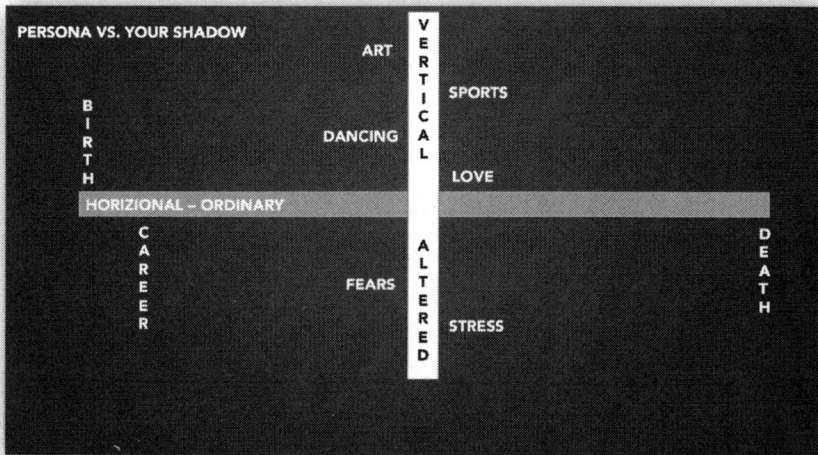

I've created this graph to illustrate just how dramatically your altered state differs from your ordinary state. We all have the ability to decide which state of consciousness we want to employ from moment to moment and from circumstance to circumstance. We can decide whether to be angry, sad, happy or glad. Disappointing things happen to all of us but the way you handle these events is what makes the difference. Someone living an authentic life says, let's get over the setback and make something good happen. They know that growth and massive change needs to happen to move forward in life. People who live in the altered state are more engaged and committed and they're more passionate because they've become their true selves. This self-awareness helps them know exactly who they are and where they're supposed to be.

Another way to illustrate this is by using a horizontal line to represent your ordinary state of consciousness. You go through life in a routine fashion: wake up in the morning, eat breakfast, go to the gym, sit in traffic, go to work, eat lunch, buy groceries, eat dinner, watch TV then go to sleep. Every single day you follow the same routine and you get used to it. Nothing special but everything seems to be working fine. Most people live in an ordinary state of consciousness and fail to tap into their altered state, which I believe is a very sad way to go through life. When you remain in your ordinary state, you stay on the horizontal line and deny yourself the opportunity to truly live life to the fullest.

Now look at your altered state of consciousness as a vertical line, when you're doing something that breaks the daily monotony. If you've ever been to a wedding and the DJ played your favorite song, you probably started to sing it out loud and dance to the beat and you didn't even care about who was watching you. You weren't thinking about routine things like what you needed from the grocery store because you were in an altered state of consciousness and were feeling more energized and in spirit.

It's like when I watch the Golden State Warriors play basketball. I have to admit that I get more than excited watching the best team in the league perform at their highest level. When Stephen Curry or Kevin Durant hit a three-pointer or when Draymond Green blocks a shot into the stands, I feel like I'm out there on the court with them and in the zone! That's me living in my altered state of consciousness. Nothing routine about sitting three rows above the world champions' bench!

My wife and I first met in 1996. When we went on our first date and then had our first kiss, I was an altered state of consciousness. I was an immature 16-year old kid but somehow I knew deep inside that she was special and unique and was the woman I needed to spend my life with. That amazing feeling played itself out when we finally got married in 2014. I realized very early in our relationship that she was the woman I wanted next to me forever. When you're aware of what you truly want and need, you're in an altered state of consciousness, living the authentic life. I don't know if there's anything more rewarding, other than my relationship with God.

PERSONA VS. SHADOW

When we spend time on social media, we typically post only the happy or funny things that occur in our lives, not the details of an argument or our financial struggles. We rarely post the entire truth about anything, only the perception that we want others to see. When we do that we are showcasing our persona. The opposite of our persona is our shadow, or, the true you.

Some people live in persona for so long they forget who they really are. Years ago I watched a movie titled Jerry Maguire. Tom Cruise played a very aggressive sports agent whose singular mindset was to make money. You've probably heard the phrase, "Show me the money!" That was Jerry Maguire's demand when he negotiated new contracts for his clients.

In one scene, one of Jerry's clients, an NHL hockey player, was seriously hurt during a game. While the player was taken off the ice, his son begged Jerry, "When are you going to tell my dad to stop playing?" Jerry told the kid that nothing could stop his dad, not even a tank. The son cursed him out and ran off because he knew Jerry was using his father only for financial gain and would drain every ounce from him as a player.

That night Jerry couldn't sleep and in the middle of the night he experienced an awakening. His shadow told him to become his father's son again and enjoy the simple pleasures of the career he loved. It was no longer his persona talking but his shadow helping him rewrite his manifesto for life and work.

Let's say you're a doctor who wants to exude a professional persona out in public. Well, there's nothing wrong with that. But there's a point when you have to set aside the attitude, especially when you're off duty. The persona of an insurance sales person may be that they can always close a deal. Your persona is how you need to present yourself to get your job done. I understand that. But if your persona dominates, you neglect your shadow. Your persona shouldn't change who you really are and, like too many others have done, allow your job to define you.

That actually happened to me when my business was exploding in a good way. All of a sudden my ego started to grow and I turned into the business, instead of remaining who I was.

That's when I asked if I had changed as a person. Do people even recognize me anymore? It's a battle that many people fight on a daily basis. When your persona takes over your shadow, you live a life that others think you should live. Please don't lose yourself in your persona. Strive to be yourself in your shadow and always make sure that what you do is authentically you.

The Rhino Mentality

Many of my friends have kidded me about writing a business book using rhinos as the central theme. But once I explain the meaning behind the RHINO acronym, people begin to understand that rhinos and humans share many similarities that highlight the visible and potential power that both possess. As I dove deeper into writing this book and developed the best way to relate a rhino philosophy to business and personal life, I felt convinced that it would be a great metaphor to help others escalate their own careers and family commitments.

Before I go any further, I must give credit to Les Schalais, a man I consider one of my mentors and the gentleman who originally introduced me to the RHINO concept. When I first heard his concept, I laughed at the idea because I thought, I'm not a rhino, I don't look like a rhino (or at least I don't think I do). But as I listened more closely to Les, I heard him carefully describe the mentality of a rhino and how we can mirror the way a rhino functions with how we conduct our business and personal lives.

THE BIG FIVE

Most people don't know this tidbit but the rhino is considered one of the animal kingdom's Big Five, the beasts that big game hunters consider the most difficult animals in Africa to hunt on foot. The trophy-worthy Big Five includes the lion, the African elephant, the buffalo, the African leopard and the rhino. These animals are skilled hunters themselves and they're the only animals in the world that will not flee when a rifle is shot at them. In fact, they will attack in the same direction from where the shot was fired. Hunters with a slow trigger finger have even been killed when attempting to get off a second shot at one of the Big Five.

So, that's why I consider the RHINO acronym such a valuable tool, because the rhino has tendencies that can be compared to how we should conduct business or how we should live our personal lives. I'll do my best to expand on this interesting acronym to help you see how it can help you grow your business and enhance your personal life.

R — stands for the ability to <u>relate</u> to what people need and want and the skill to help them get it.

H — stands for <u>helping</u> others get to where they want to go in business and coaching them to reach their goals and dreams.

I — stands for <u>inspiring</u> others to greatness by setting a great example.

N — stands for <u>nurturing</u> others, listening with empathy and guiding them to success.

O — stands for striving to help as many <u>others</u> as possible.

I believe it's very inspiring when you use the RHINO acronym as a reminder to Relate, Help, Inspire and Nurture Others throughout your business and personal life. It's a wonderful way to describe the true Rhino Mentality that I have adopted for this book, for my business and for my overall approach to life itself.

A RHINO IS VALUABLE

Rhinos are very rare, which makes them extremely valuable creatures. In contrast, there aren't very many people who view themselves as being rare. Instead, most people describe themselves as ordinary, typical or just average. The sad thing about that is they fail to tap into their true potential, maybe because of past failures or circumstances that they might not have had control over. In many cases, people have heard others speak negatively about them and have associated themselves with failure.

When you have the RHINO mentality, you understand that you are rare and extremely valuable. You were put on this earth to do something special and I believe every day you should be actively pursuing that something. I believe we're all given gifts and your biggest responsibility is discovering what that gift is and sharing it with the world.

Most people in the traditional work force hold a 9-to-5 job and there's nothing wrong with that. I'm just saying that most 9-to-5 people get tired of doing the same thing over and over again every single day. But that's because they fail to tap in to their rare gifts. For example, a guy gets up in the morning, eats his standard breakfast, gets into his standard car and makes the standard commute to his standard office. He goes through the motions at work for eight hours then has to commute the opposite way home. When he gets home he's so tired he wolfs down a microwave dinner and watches TV shows that entertain but don't inspire him. I don't think there's anything wrong with entertainment but I also believe that it's hard to have multi-million dollar ideas when you're putting garbage into your mind every evening. I do think it's important that we are careful about what we allow into our minds, whether it be through TV, radio or social media.

Now I know everybody has days when they just need to rest or other days when they want to let loose and have fun. But I think when you feed yourself, you should do it as if you're a rare and valuable thoroughbred. If you know you are valuable you will treat yourself differently. You'll see yourself differently. You'll act differently. When you see yourself act differently, you'll feel differently and you'll get different results. But it all goes back to the question: do you realize how rare and valuable you really are?

As valuable and rare as rhinos are, we are even more priceless. We must truly believe that we can make our lives anything we want by acknowledging that we are truly rare and extremely valuable.

A RHINO HAS THICK SKIN
Rhinos have a unique skin, approximately two inches thick and nearly impossible for its enemies to penetrate. Business people who have a RHINO mentality also possess a very thick skin. They

don't take things personally, they don't get bothered, they don't get discouraged and they aren't annoyed by others. They try not to get fazed by things they can't control. Most people have difficulty handling these pressures but as we develop the RHINO mentality and those issues attack us from all directions, that's when we have the opportunity to demonstrate just how thick our skin can be.

I lost my mother when she was 44 years old. I was only ten when she passed away and I just couldn't imagine how things were going to be without her for the rest of my life. If you've lost your mother you know exactly what I mean. I considered myself a mama's boy because I was very spoiled by her. She took care of me and we were extremely close. Mom was my life and losing her took a lot out of me. I had to grow the thick skin that would be able to handle holidays without my mom, especially when I saw my friends whose moms were still living. Back then I thought they were very fortunate and that I was the unlucky one. Eventually you have to develop strength inside of you plus that thick skin. Although it feels terrible in the beginning, over time you get stronger. I use my Mom's memory as a way to inspire me to do great things. If I had let her passing allow me to feel sorry for myself, I never would have grown into the man I believe I was meant to be.

I've also operated businesses where people violated my trust. You know, it's interesting. Sometimes you think you have great friends and trustworthy business partners—you may even call them your brothers and sisters—but when it comes down to money and business, you can often be disappointed. Many times I trusted business people who I thought were going to work well with me and I wouldn't have to worry about turning my back on them. But I've been disappointed so many times. I had to learn that people have their own agendas, whether in business or friendship, and you need to have thick skin to handle what people will sometimes do to you.

You will feel discouraged when someone betrays you in business. You may not know how to move forward because you're trying to fathom the reason they did damage to you. But you have a choice to either be shocked or paralyzed by the setback or to be strong and thick-skinned like a RHINO. Don't get discouraged or let things bother you because this too shall pass.

A RHINO CAN SMELL

Rhinos have a keen sense of smell, which I compare to business instincts and a keen work ethic. You can't just get lucky; you have to work hard to make things happen. As you work, you can feel it in your core that this is who you are. You can smell that something good is going to happen and you have this gut feeling that success is coming your way. I don't care what your past has been; you need to cultivate the feeling that things are going to work out well.

Do you remember that time you drove into a parking lot and said to yourself, I'm going to find a parking space, then all of a sudden, bam, a parking space came up? Or, have you ever wished for something great to happen and all of a sudden it did? I've read books and watched movies about the Law of Attraction, which is a theory about visualizing and attracting things into your life

Some people don't believe in the Law of Attraction but I do. I believe you are what you think about every single day. If you think negatively, you'll attract the negative. If you think positively, you'll attract the positive.

A rhino has a keen sense of smell and I believe a RHINO should have a keen and positive work ethic. Seeing the world as a positive place will affect your life in a positive way and help you leave a lasting legacy with family, friends and others you come in contact with.

A RHINO IS TOUGH

Rhinos are extremely tough and they will attack anyone or anything that tries to hurt them. In business you also need to be extremely tough. You may not necessarily be physically attacked but if you're a RHINO you will protect your life, your family, your clients and the business that you built.

Rhinos on a rampage can destroy anything in their path. In business, that means destroying opposition, competition, resistance or any challenges that stand between you and your goals. If you want to get to a certain place in your life you need to have the mentality that nothing is going to stop you. You are going to do it no matter what, even when you don't want to do it anymore. You have the discipline to do it every single day even when the initial excitement that you enjoyed when you began is gone.

Each year people are excited about getting in shape for the New Year but right around February or March that feeling vanishes. To be successful at anything in life, you've got to get past the excitement stage and learn discipline and consistency. A rhino on a rampage will destroy everything in its path. A person with the RHINO mentality can achieve anything because they're focused, committed and disciplined to not let anything stop them.

A RHINO CAN PUSH

If you challenge rhinos, they will push back hard. I compare that to business competition that breeds success. I'm a huge sports fan and it's a pleasure to watch the best athletes in the world challenge each other at the highest level of competition. It's awesome to be able to see athletes who are so hungry to win and I know that same mentality works in the business world. When you're faced with opposition from a strong competitor, develop the mindset that you'll charge harder until you achieve your victory.

I believe competition brings out the best in all of us. Rhinos strike fear in any enemy that challenges them. Even a lion, the so-called King of the Jungle, is scared of a rhino. You have to answer the question: who's the lion in your life? Who's that lion in your business? Sometimes that lion can be your own fears and the limitations in your own mind. We need to look at our life and say, you know what, I'm going to beat that lion. I'm going to put fear into my lions so they disappear.

A RHINO mentality calls for you to charge harder, attack your fears and do what you fear most. If public speaking scares you, attack the fear and do it. If you're scared to sit in front of a prospect one-on-one, attack the fear and do it. Push back on your fears like a RHINO.

A RHINO IS FEARLESS

You have probably figured out by now that rhinos are fearless and will take on the fiercest animals in the jungle if they are provoked. You, too, must look at your business and personal life as if nothing will affect or intimidate you. You've got to be fearless. Being an entrepreneur may be new and you might be facing the true fear of failure. But you can overcome that and become fearless like a rhino in a way that motivates you to push through every hurdle to get the job done. You discover that it's an amazing feeling and a great testimony to the RHINO mentality when you are finally able to overcome your greatest fears or conquer self-imposed limitations.

Stages of Endurance

To be a RHINO you need to have the ability to endure through tough times because they are guaranteed to come. After so many years of experience in this business, I've learned that there are three stages that someone must go through in order to even think about getting to the highest level of success.

1. Number one is the stage where you fool yourself. You say to yourself that it's going to happen but deep inside you don't really believe it. In this early stage you've let your doubts take over and you know 100% that you're going to leave the business. You chant affirmations, "I'm going to do it, I'm going to do it, I'm going to do it." But, in the back of your mind, you know you're not. That stage is tough to get through.

2. The second stage is when most people just give up. "You know what, I'm out, I don't want to do this anymore." When it starts to get tough or challenging they just quit. They get into something new and then a couple of months later they're out again. They start up a new diet or a get-rich-quick program but they fail to finish. My business is insurance based and we had to pass exams to get a license. Many people who fail the test quit after one try. When I first took that test I did not pass. The second time I took it I did not pass. The third time I took it I did not pass. Four times I took it and did not pass. I almost left after the fourth miss, thinking that maybe I just had a studying problem. I didn't pass it until the fifth time but I had told myself I was not going to give up. I was not going to fail the quitting phase. I kept going and kept pushing until I passed the test. It may have taken me two years to pass my insurance exam but my career changed after that and I've never looked back. I can tell you right now, the best thing that ever happened to me was flunking that exam but when I was flunking it was hard on my ego. I would sit in front of the mirror and ask, what's wrong with me? I had friends who were passing that test on the first try. When they told me that it was really easy it would make me feel like an idiot but I would never give up. What's amazing is that those friends who passed it on the first try are not even in the industry anymore. They quit.

3. So, while they passed the test, they took it for granted and as the years progressed they quit because they couldn't get through the third stage, the endurance stage. Can you handle it when things get tough? Can you handle it when it becomes a real business? It's not always going to be beautiful. It's not always going to be sunny outside. It's not always going to be a great day in business. Business has lots of ups and downs and many have a difficult time handling the endurance stage and most just give up. My challenge to you is, whatever you have to go through, get through the endurance stage. Anybody can deal with the ups but can you endure the downs? When it's hard, that's when you discover your endurance level. If you understand that this is an endurance contest, you'll want to be a RHINO who is able to endure.

LEARN BY DOING

You could read a book about learning to swim but it's not until you jump into the pool that you figure out how to do it. The key is to learn as you do it and know that you're going to make mistakes and go through ups and downs. As I said, it's going to be an endurance test. In team building, selling is only two percent of the process. Understanding people and your product is the other 98%. If you understand your product and people, that's the secret sauce. Make sure that you understand the power of the product that you offer and determine to know what people really need and want.

RECRUITING

Many people try to learn sales skills and develop tactics to convince someone to make a purchase. I contend that, if you care about people and understand your product, you're going to dwarf someone who's a great salesperson. Understand that recruiting and team building is a numbers business. Not everyone's going to buy from you or want to work in your business but some will. The ones you're looking for are the ones who want an opportunity and are hungry for it.

Recruiting is not forcing or convincing someone to join. They're either going to want to do it or not. All you can really do is share an idea that hopefully triggers something in them and they get excited about building a business with you. Since this is a numbers business, the more people you meet and talk to and the more references you collect, the more positive relationships you will build. I want to share one very important reminder: just because they don't work with you doesn't mean you can't be friends. A no doesn't mean you can't hang out with them anymore. I've always been amazed by people who like you if you work with them but don't like you if you don't work with them. We're in a free enterprise world where you're going to have competition, people selling the same product or business model. Why can't everyone just get along?

I've seen this happen so many times when a friend decides to go another direction and all of a sudden they're not friends anymore. Don't lose friendships because you can't work together. Think of the bigger picture. I believe in loyalty, integrity and doing things right. You cannot force someone to see your vision or stay in the same business with you. You can only hope that they want to keep working with you and they share that vision for a long time. But it doesn't mean you can't be friends or hang out or go to movies and have dinner with each other.

It's amazing but I've seen that many times in my career. Not only will they not want to hang around with you but they'll also talk behind your back or start rumors to get an edge over you. I don't worry about backstabbing or bad mouthing. I'm a Christian so I don't worry about things of that nature because it isn't my battle. I just focus on what I can control. You're not really competing against people who are doing the wrong thing with bad intentions or who don't work hard. You're really competing with the ten percent who work hard and do what's right. Doing the right thing and working hard is the simple secret for taking your business to the next level.

My Philosophy

I was not raised in a sales environment. I began as a customer service representative in the claims department. If you were in a car accident you were given my number to contact so that I could get your car fixed. I got used to working a service-based job so I wasn't really aggressive about becoming well known. I just wanted to get the job done and go home. I don't think there's anything wrong with that. In fact, I thought I was very fortunate to have a job.

But as an entrepreneur you have competitors who are very aggressive on social media, whether it is YouTube, Twitter, Instagram or Snapchat. Twenty years ago, you would consider buying TV commercials or advertising in the local newspaper. But no matter the era, people need to know that your business exists. You can't operate as a "secret agent."

So, as I prepare my yearly goals, dreams and plans, I always make sure to keep three things in mind: become more known, challenge myself and transform.

1. BECOME WELL-KNOWN

One of the big challenges that sales people face is the perception of the career field by those on the outside. Greedy, pushy or cheesy is how many people would describe sales agents. In my world, though, insurance is more a business of serving people, not sales. When you're serving someone, there's no reason why you should feel bad to become better known or to promote yourself to help your business earn more money. Some people adhere to the philosophy that money is a bad thing, the root of all evil or something that turns someone into a bad person. I would challenge that assumption by saying that money doesn't necessarily make you a bad person but it does magnify whom you are inside. If you make lots of money and you're a great person you're a great person when you make lots of money. If you're not such a great person money may magnify that you're not such a great person. If you're a big show-off when you don't have a lot of money you're probably going to be a big show-off when you do have money. But if you're humble when you don't have money you'll probably still be humble when you have money. It comes down to the question of mindset. What limiting belief is holding you back from being better known, for being more confident and excited about what you do and for being more passionate about your job?

2. CHALLENGE

Every day of the year you're going to be challenged. Many people have a false belief that things should always be easy but I believe you must accept being challenged. I hired a personal trainer because I wanted to take my health to another level. I had been going to the gym to do the same boring exercises but I soon found out that I was in a rut. But when a trainer starts to work on different body parts, your body is challenged in new and different ways. On the very first day my trainer had me doing exercises that I'd never done before and he put me through the rigors without mercy.

The morning after my first workout I was so sore that I could barely walk. But I went into it expecting to be challenged and I expected to be sore. I knew it was going to be hard because challenge is how you grow and how you take life to the next level. When you decide to join a business and work for yourself, accept the fact that it's going to be hard. Accept the fact that not everyone is going to be able to handle it. Accept the fact that you're going to get challenged by things that are beyond what you've ever gone through. Knowing that challenges are coming makes it easier when they happen. Wanting to be challenged is a major and positive belief system. You've got to tell your mind that you're going to be ready for the challenge when it comes your way, because it will.

3. TRANSFORM

I believe that you should be transformed every year to grow into a better version of yourself. A caterpillar goes into a cocoon for a short period of time and emerges as an entirely different animal. It's now a butterfly! Being in the cocoon led to a major transformation.

I recommend that you go into your own cocoon. Allow your body and your mindset to change and stop walking or crawling through life. It's now time to fly! What you've learned so far has gotten you to where you are but you need to go into a cocoon for a time so that you can be transformed and spread your wings and fly to the next level.

LIVING THROUGH CHANGE

I live in the San Francisco Bay Area where a six-figure income is now considered "low to moderate income." When I was brought up a six-figure income was a big deal. Back in the 80s, the average income was around $17-grand a year. So if you made $100k you were in a small percentage of those who made big money. Now $100,000 is considered a "paltry" living and that makes for an interesting challenge. But that's the way things are now and we must adapt to change whether we like it or not.

I always look back at things that were so different only a decade ago. Today we have Donald Trump as the President of the United States but I remember him on The Apprentice. I used to watch him fire people and today he's the most powerful man on the planet. I also see that people are addicted to their cell phones, tablets or computers. I remember when I used to call my wife and needed to ask for an "emergency break" to get through a busy signal. Today you have call waiting and 3-way calling. I remember my relatives used to call the Philippines at a very expensive rate. Today those calls are all free with Viber and you can even see them on Skype. It's amazing how things have changed.

I remember just a few years ago when we used to record our favorite music from the radio by using the lousy record microphone

on a tape player. Today you have all the music you could ever imagine streaming online. It's just a different world today and I bring that up as a reminder that we have to be ready for change and adapt to it.

I hear people who lean on the excuse that they're "old school," meaning that they don't want to adjust to change; they want to use what's gotten them there. Some old school things make complete sense, like love or commitment or being romantic. But if you don't adapt to change in business, you could become a dinosaur. Things are moving so fast that, by the time my daughter has children, she'll be buying self-driving cars. I guarantee there's going to be many more changes that you must adapt to so don't be left behind.

WHAT MOVES ME?

Every year, I ask, "What really moves me"? The first thing I think about is how I look at the world. Some people live in what they call their "stuck." They've reached a certain point in their life and they believe that's all they're going to get to. They feel trapped or bored. They have a routine but they really don't strive as much as they used to and they feel like their best years are behind them. It's almost like being caged or trapped. People get to this point because they're not spontaneous or easily excited anymore. They could be very defensive if you present an opportunity to them because they don't want to change the routine of their life. They see no growth or change because they're trapped and it's sad because they're living with a prisoner mentality.

"You just don't understand what I'm going through."
"You just don't understand my situation."
"You just don't understand my life."

I bet all of us could find excuses for why we're not where we want to be. But to get to where you want to go you can't be trapped in a self-imposed prison or a cage. You have to grow and get out of that and adapt to change. Maybe you don't want to adapt to change because you're stuck in your old belief systems. Or maybe you believe everything's OK already and you're just very comfortable and satisfied.

Maybe when you were a kid you were sold on the philosophy that you were supposed to go to school, get a good job, get married and buy a house and a golf membership. If you do all those things that's cool and you feel great about your life. All the pieces of your puzzle are in place and you really don't have any complaints because this is what you thought life would be. But is it possible that you could have all the things on your checklist and still not be happy or fulfilled? I see it all the time and know that's true.

MONETIZE YOUR PASSION

When it comes to business, am I doing something that I truly love? Can I monetize it so that my family and I can enjoy a comfortable lifestyle? Here's my own opinion about hobbies and passions. Many people will do something just because they love doing it and they believe that just because they love doing it, they should be able to monetize it. But not all things that I love to do turn into money. I truly love to play basketball but I'm a 5'10" Filipino and I didn't make it to a great college so my chances of being on a professional basketball team run from extremely small to less than zero. Although it's a passion of mine it's never going to monetize. I realized early that whatever I love to do I should be able to monetize because I need to make a living for my family.

I could still play basketball every single day because you can live out your passions for free. I play basketball and don't need to make money off it because I love doing it. But in business you have to find a way to monetize your passions so that you'll love doing what you do every single day and be excited to wake up for it. I run a business where I get to help people. I sell life insurance and work with great team members and we love to build and develop new entrepreneurs. There's nothing more exciting than seeing a person develop the business they love doing. I often remind people that I lost my mom at a young age and fully realize the value of life insurance so that's why there was such a burning passion to get involved in this arena of business.

PAST, PRESENT OR FUTURE?

In any given moment you're probably thinking about what you've done in the past, crying over spilled milk or imagining what the future will hold. Rarely are people living in the present moment. Most people get stuck thinking about the past, which they have no control of. You can learn from the past but to constantly dwell on it doesn't serve you as much as being in the present. As for the future, you're not even promised tomorrow. You should be living in the now because when you're present, you're truly alive.

When you're present it's like being on your first date. You're not thinking about going home because you're so excited that you don't want to let go. That's a great example to remind us that we can only control what we're doing right now. Life is an interesting journey and when you're younger it goes by pretty slowly. When I was a kid I couldn't wait to turn sixteen so I could drive a car and then I couldn't wait till I was 18 so I could go into nightclubs and then when I was 21 so that I could drink and have certain rights as an adult. But when you get into your 30s and 40s life starts to move a little faster. You finish high school, go to college, buy your first home and get married, then all of a sudden you have children and then grandchildren and then you look at retirement and traveling and the final segment of your lifetime. These days we're living to about 80 or 90 and in the next few decades people may reach into the hundreds. Regardless, this life is very precious and it goes by very quickly. Don't waste it living outside of the now.

FOCUS

One of the challenges that we face is the inability to focus. We live in a world where things are happening so fast, our attention span has dropped to about eight seconds. I read somewhere that two hours worth of distractions happen to us each day. That means that every eleven minutes you'll be distracted by something. If you want to take your life and your business to another level, you need to learn how to focus. I would prefer a person who can focus over someone with a high IQ because of their ability to block out distractions and be effective.

Focus and the ability to handle distractions is a critical piece of the RHINO mentality. Run in a straight line and you'll see yourself achieving the dreams and goals you've always wanted.

ERASING DOUBT

What do you want in your life? What do you want to happen today? How do you want to make an impact? Many of us have ideas and goals and dreams that we want to see come to fruition. You may put more emphasis on your family, or your health, or job, your spiritual life or charity works. Regardless, the intention is to live a complete life that is authentically yours and to make an impact. The number one course of action is eliminating your self-doubt.

I suffered with doubt early in life. It was like the cartoons with the angel on one shoulder and the devil on the other. They're both talking to you and you're not sure which one to listen to. Since I didn't go to college, I didn't have any technical skills so I doubted myself all the time. Because of my background I thought I was going to have limited options. When you feel doubt, you wind up paralyzing yourself.

I thought doubt was only for people who were failing but I now realize that even the most successful people have faced doubts. There are many who have risen above the doubts because they learned to focus. When you minimize the self-doubt, you put yourself in position for a great life. What I recommend to eliminate self-doubt is to get up and move. Focus on what you want to achieve and make something happen immediately. Take action that moment. When you're busy moving forward, it's harder for self-doubt to attack.

Find a mentor who you trust and who has results to show. A mentor doesn't have to be the richest person you know. In fact, I never chase after the wealthiest guys. Instead, I look for someone who overcame a challenge that is similar to mine.

LEAVE A LEGACY

Instead of living out the ugly traits above, leave a legacy of what you did to serve others. Instead of trying to prove that you're the smartest person in the room be the one who helps others find their true potential. As the great Zig Ziglar used to teach, utilize your wisdom, time and talent to help other people get to where they want to go in life.

Wisdom is learned through a series of experiences and decisions, both good and bad. The world is tough and I prefer to have empathy for what other people go through. You should also encourage others to be strong and courageous, face their fears and be inspired to get to the next level. Write a book about your life and leave a legacy. Maybe someone who reads it will have it affect his or her life in a positive way.

People are not always going to understand or see things from your perspective. Not everyone's going to believe in the things that you believe in even though you may be saying things from your heart. You can't please everybody but you should respect other people's opinions. You are a magnet, either attracting other people into your space or repelling them.

There are a number of human traits that I'll pinpoint and urge you to avoid at all cost.

1. **Selfishness** - Selfish people always need to have everything their way. Those with a selfish mentality think that the world revolves around them and that they should be entitled to all privileges.

2. **Know it All** - We all fight that battle. You've read an article about the ten reasons for this or that and now you're an expert. We stop studying because we become know-it-alls and because information comes so fast and easily.

3. **Center of Attention** - We all battle the ego, the inside person that thinks the world revolves around them. When your ego is driving, it always wants to be the center of attention. When someone is chasing attention they'll always make sure a conversation turns into something about them.

4. **Smartest Person** - I read a quote that says, "If you're the smartest person in the room you're in the wrong room." You may have 90 years to prove that you're the smartest person in the room but there's going to be more generations of smarter people to follow.

Winning Habits of a RHINO

Throughout my sales career, no matter what business I was in, I always took ownership. I was never "in somebody else's business" even though at times I was under someone who owned the business. Regardless, I always took ownership as if it was my own company. I didn't want to feel as if someone was on my back saying, you have to do this, you have to do that. I just decided to outwork myself and I treated the business as if I had invested half a million dollars into it and I wanted to get my money back. Even if you didn't start your business with a lot of money, assume that you put a lot into it because your time is at least as valuable as your money.

In fact, I consider time to be more important than money so I've always had a sense of urgency to make things happen. I've always believed that whatever business I was in was the last great opportunity so I have to go all out. This business I'm in is the last one, the one I'm going to put my heart into. Treat every opportunity as if it's your last. If you don't work hard and go all out, you will likely see yourself fail because you've set such a low standard.

BUILD FOR THE FUTURE

In our business, you don't get paid today for what you do today. What you do today pays off down the road so you want to make sure that you spend time wisely. Today's work becomes the foundation of your business. You want to give yourself about two years to form good habits are and determine how legitimate your business is. Use that time to develop a flow and gain momentum. Most people want it fast but, as my old mentor said, you need to go slow to go fast. Take your time to do it right, go step by step and don't cut corners. It could take time before you start to get the business into your bloodstream but it will happen if you remember the key: go slow to go fast.

For those who do what I do, there are only two ways to make money. One is by prospecting new clients and making sales. The second is by prospecting for new agents who would like to work with me. Getting more people to jump into the battle with me has always been the foundation of my business because the bigger you get the more you can leverage yourself. I love the concept of leverage because, when you work alone you only make money when you make a sale, but when you've leveraged yourself, hundreds or thousands of partners help you make the most of your time. Less effort, more return.

That's why I've always loved the concept of team building. Team building is the most fun and allows you to make a bigger impact on people. Say you have a friend who has a full-time job but he hates the hours or he's outgrown his position or missed a promotion. Whatever the case may be, teach him my business and he can turn that part-time income into a full-time career and change his entire life.

It's fun to watch that scenario unfold but it takes time for it to happen. As someone with the RHINO mentality, be the lead person and show someone how they can make money and generate an income. That's extremely important when people first join the business. Most people coming into a new business need to make an income quickly so you need to show them a path to that security. Team building has many moving parts—leadership, teamwork, fun, inspiration and motivation—so many different things that are so exciting and rewarding.

POSITIVE ATTITUDE

One of my favorite bits of advice is to always have a positive attitude, no matter what. That's always tough but I urge you to maintain a positive attitude and outlook on life, a positive perception of other people and a positive knowledge that great things will happen to you. In the past, I always assumed that bad things were going to happen and after my mother passed away I asked, "Why does that have to happen to me?" But years later I started changing my paradigm to, "What great things are going to happen to me? What amazing things can happen today?" Having a positive attitude is keeping up the communication with yourself, expecting great results and the knowledge that the best of things for you and your family are coming your way.

WORK HARD

Some people work hard at being lazy. Some people have never worked hard so they don't even know what it looks like. They've never felt the pain of sacrifice and dedication. To become successful, it's necessary to work hard. Hard work can outdo talent. Talent is God-given; some people are great communicators, some are great at strategy and others can sell ice to an Eskimo. They're so amazing that most of us could work hard all our lives and still not be as good as the person who utilizes their gift. But I've also learned that hard work can dwarf talent when the gifted person takes it for granted and cuts corners.

One of the misconceptions is that talent doesn't have to work hard. Actually, I believe it's completely opposite. I think talent needs to work harder because the temptation to ease up is stronger and you must avoid that lure. It's similar to a basketball team that knows how good they are so they wait until the fourth quarter before turning it on. They assume they'll catch up but if they wait too long the other team may get hot and win the game. It's the same in business. Some people say, I'll be bigger than this guy or I'll have more sales or blah, blah, blah. But they're leaning on talent, which may not generate the positive results that they took for granted.

DEDICATION

Some people are only dedicated or committed until they lose the excitement, when they stop doing the fun part or have that feeling of newness wash away. You need to be dedicated to your business long after you're excited about it. That means that even when you're not as excited you'll still keep going. Dedication and commitment means going through the tough times, going through the down-markets and battling through your areas of struggle. Be dedicated to your business through the ups and downs.

BE UNCOMFORTABLE
Along those same lines, I was trained that success can be uncomfortable. Don't wait around hoping that somebody will invent a comfortable way to make an income. There's never going to be a day when someone's going to invent a business where you do absolutely nothing and you can sit at home and be bored while you're getting rich. You're fooling yourself if you believe that sales or team building is comfortable. I think that trying to rise to the next level is uncomfortable. It takes you out of a comfort zone, out of a normal schedule. Whatever you've done, your life has gotten you to a certain point and if you want more then you're going to have to do something outside of what you've been doing. You have to work in an uncomfortable state to appreciate what you're doing.

ADJUST TO CHANGE
I mentioned my personal trainer named Rich, who has me do things that I'm not used to doing and it can be extremely uncomfortable. But the body gets used to it and adjusts until he teaches me the next round of new exercises. I believe we have to look at our business in a similar way. If it's too comfortable, sometimes

you'll do less. One way to determine if you're comfortable is how you were led to believe life was meant to be. When I was growing up I was taught that you have to go to the right school and get good grades then go to college and get a degree. When you get your degree you apply for a job and stay there for many years and hopefully get promoted a few times before you retire.

It was a simple mindset about what life is supposed to be. I was even told that life is a routine and it would always be boring. These things were stuck in my mind when I was a child but deep inside I knew that wasn't the way it should be. I didn't graduate from college and I always felt that I would struggle because of what I was told as a kid. But you can't determine the heart or the drive in an individual. You can't determine what moves someone. If a person is hungry to get to the next level in their life there's nothing that can stop them and we need to help people understand that if they're committed and dedicated they can find a way.

I'm not saying it's going to be easy and you may have been brought up in a culture without certain advantages. I totally understand, but for the most part, if you really push and move forward deliberately, you can find yourself going closer to your goals and dreams. I think most people just give up because they believe they've reached what they were supposed to be. I got married, great. I got my car, great. I got my kids, great. I got my house, great. I guess I should just live it out now. If you live like everything is comfortable how do you reach the next level? What if there's another level that you've never tapped into because you were so comfortable at your current level?

Is it possible there's a higher version of yourself that you haven't tapped into? If you believe you've reached the highest level, congratulations. But I believe there's always another level, whether it's mental or physical, whether it's a relationship with your spouse or becoming better at your craft or just becoming a more congruent individual. That requires a greater you to take over.

MAKE YOUR MONEY WORK

When you make money don't be so caught up with having to spend it right away or flaunting it and don't get so caught up in wanting to accumulate things. Many people just want to make money to buy a lot of things so they wind up buying things they don't need. I believe there's got to be a controlling mindset that says you can't buy everything. Instead, put money away for a retirement goal or to help your children or to just have peace of mind about money. If you've ever gone through a situation where you didn't have any money, which I have, you appreciate when you have something you can lean on. You've got to put something away so that if things don't work out the way you've expected, you're prepared. So make your money work for you. I'm not saying you can't enjoy your money because what's the point of making it if you can't enjoy it? I like traveling with my wife and my family. I like sports and buy tickets to watch our local teams. I love experiences but you still have to put money to work for you and make sure that you're being disciplined about how you spend it.

BE HAPPY

There is a difference between saying I feel good, everything's great, everything's going to work out and genuinely being happy about the things in your life. In sales and team building, many people fail to take time to be happy about their business. Sometimes you get so fixated on achieving the goal that you don't realize how much fun you could be having in-between. Sometimes the greatest part is the process. When I married my wife we were so excited for the wedding day but it was also fun preparing for the wedding. It was fun taking the engagement photos, going to rehearsal dinners, looking for my wife's dress and picking the right photographer.

When they're building a business most people tend to connect it to making X amount of money, needing a certain number of team members in their organization or meeting a certain goal before they can truly enjoy the business and be happy. I would like to challenge that and encourage you to enjoy the process of building a business because you learn a lot through the ups and the downs. You get to meet a lot of people and see different types of personalities. In a team building business one of the most underestimated things is the challenge of keeping everyone together to reach all your objectives and goals.

We underestimate the power in that process. Enjoy the fact that people see things differently. You can't allow your ego to dictate that everyone must see things your way. Being happy in any situation is the essence of a big team builder, so be happy and love what you do.

Give It Up!

When I speak to people I'm training, I often use the term "give it up." What I'm referring to is leaving behind certain habits or conditions that you might be accustomed to in order to improve your own performance and build a team with the RHINO mentality. I'll use the next few pages to give you some ideas and tips about things that you should give up if you are sincere about building a big organization and fielding a team that will want to follow you to the top and continue to strive for greatness.

UNHEALTHY DIET

Building a team can take a physical toll on you so I've always believed that your first priority should be giving up an unhealthy diet or lifestyle. Our business often requires evening meetings and sometimes hours of driving to get there. The business also requires focus. But if things get too hectic, you could find yourself eating things that aren't good for you, whether it be fast food, sugary drinks or salty snacks. I love hamburgers and fries but when I decided to get in shape, I had to learn how to take it easy. Those food items will not promote your best health and over time they'll take their toll on your body. Give up on those types of foods and boost your daily physical activity.

I'm not going to get into what you specifically need to eat or which eating program works the best. I'm just saying that a healthy diet serves you well and helps you be more of what you want to be. The benefits are obvious and can transform you almost overnight. Healthy eating gives you energy, helps you get the right amount of rest, saves you from daily stress and ensures that you're refueling your body with the food that it needs. Go to any bookstore from here to there and you'll find shelves filled with health books and philosophies. Pick the one that's right one for you and stick to the plan.

While you're at it, increase your daily walking distance with your dog, ride your bike for a couple of miles each day and learn how to meditate, relax and live for the moment.

PLAYING SMALL

The second priority is to begin looking at the big picture and give up your habit of playing small. I define playing small as retaining the belief that great things are only supposed to happen to other people. You must have the belief that you can turn your dreams into reality and that you possess the power to unleash your true potential. You can't be afraid of failure. On the contrary, you should be afraid to not succeed. Many people go out on a limb and create a small goal that is easy to reach. And, to their credit, they reach it. At least they achieved that much. Some people don't even have enough vision to create a small, reachable goal. But, I'm encouraging you to stretch even higher. Give up playing small because I truly believe that big things can happen to you!

EXCUSES

One of my mentors once told me that I should start keeping a log of people's excuses so that when someone gave me one I would be able to look down the list and say, "Oh, that's excuse number 45." Most people make excuses and often let those excuses take over their business and personal lives. There are plenty of excuses that many of us use when faced with the prospect of commitment. But in all honesty, those excuses could be holding you back from going where you really want to go.

> "Well, I can't do this because I have to go somewhere."
> "I've never done that before."
> "No one's ever helped me before."
> "I don't have a business background."
> "I'm not good at taking exams."
> "I didn't go to the right school."
> "I wasn't brought up on the right side of the tracks."
> "I was brought up in a tough neighborhood."
> "I just don't have the time."

The time that you need to put into your business is a commitment that sometimes goes beyond a regular 8-hour day. Your old schedule got you to where you are now, but you'll need to adjust it to get to where you want to be. That new schedule may be completely different and uncomfortable so watch out for excuses that may start popping up.

I don't care where your starting point is and I don't care what your weaknesses are. I don't care what your past failures have been. It doesn't matter. What matters is that you eliminate the excuses and begin to grow. I recommend that you take charge of your life and all of its experiences because there will soon be a great victory for you. Own the fact that you were brought up on the "wrong side of the tracks." Own the fact that your family couldn't afford to send you to the greatest university. Own the fact that you didn't have both parents around as you grew up. Whatever the case may be, own it so that when you have victory it'll feel that much more rewarding.

QUICK FIX

I stopped having the lottery mentality years ago. That's the feeling that many people have that they can rely on luck to succeed.

Give up the expectation that there is a magic pill or a get-rich-quick formula or that this business is easy and success is going to happen overnight. Maybe you were one of those who joined a new business in the past but when it got tough you quit. I've learned that success is a process which is sometimes really slow but it speeds up as your commitment, dedication and focus expand. There is no fast way to anything, whether it's in your business or your personal life. Every successful entrepreneur takes time to invest in the process, takes time to study the product and takes time to grow the business.

I'm a faith-based person and believe that some things just happen the way they happen. But you have to initiate and be aggressive and be crystal clear on what you want. If you don't know what you want, how are you going to get it? If you think about what it takes to enjoy a great relationship with your children, you know it means years of attention, communication, discipline and learning. It takes years to foster a great marriage, years of spending time together, years of communication, years of struggle and years of ups and downs. You don't just wake up and all of a sudden say, "Hey, we have a great marriage!" But in the end, it's all those years that you and your spouse invested into each other that created a great and lasting marriage.

Give up on getting lucky and go out and make things happen.

PERFECTION

My father was an over thinker and I picked up the trait from him. My wife Emily never seems to worry. She has this wonderful gift of letting things go and as I watched how it served her life, it was a lesson for me to stop overthinking. I needed to stop the "what if" scenarios in my mind because I was overthinking all the draining negative thoughts. I've learned to just stop it and go one step at a time.

I also gave up on insisting that everything needs to be perfect before taking action. I've always been taught that if I need everything to be perfect before I start a business, I'll never start. If there were a project I had to do perfectly, I wouldn't do it at all. Sometimes you've just got to stumble through mistakes, work through your confusion and move forward. Just take action and if you don't see the right results, readjust. Remember, a result is still a result and that result, good or bad, could very well lead to success.

Most people define success as the achievement of a certain goal but you can be successful even if you failed, if you learn what not to do. Then you can take a different path and appreciate the knowledge that you've gained. If you believe everything needs to be perfect, you may be setting your expectations too high and quit immediately out of frustration when something tough goes against you. Give up on the need for perfection and focus on doing what it takes one day at a time. You're going to learn many valuable lessons along the way.

CONTROL

I had to learn to give up on things that I have zero control of like the weather or politics. If you have no control of something there's no point in worrying about it. Not everyone's going to believe what you believe or see the point of view that you see or root for the team that you root for and that's OK. Everyone has their own opinion, their own journey and their own information and they're not always going to agree with you. You can do your best to try to convince them but convincing is a very stressful activity so try to let it go. I can vote for my candidate of choice but I live in San Francisco and Washington DC is a long ways away so I can only control what I can control.

As an entrepreneur you're in business for yourself but not by yourself. Most people don't grasp that concept because they believe that they need to do everything for the business to succeed. They want to lead the meetings and put all the programs together but they wind up working all aspects of their business and controlling everything. But sometimes you have to delegate control and understand that you're not going to grow if you don't spread out the work. When you build something, focus on your strengths and what you're great at. For example, maybe you're not the greatest at team training or explaining the product. You can delegate that to someone who is better at those tasks while you focus on what you're great at. Don't get me wrong, you should master your craft and learn each area of your business but you should also delegate the jobs that you're not good at to someone who does them well. They will enjoy the work, save you time and help you build your business faster.

OVER COMMITMENT

If you believe you have to do everything immediately and handle it all yourself, you will wind up getting burned out. Burnout can create excess stress and severe sickness, kill your business and generate many other negative issues. Most successful people I've talked to have learned how to say no to certain tasks, activities, demands, family, friends and colleagues in favor of accomplishing their key business goals. The fact is that most people who call you want you to support their own agenda. So, don't say yes when you really mean no if the request is not supporting your business goals, dreams and vision.

TOXIC PEOPLE

Possibly the most important thing to add to the "give it up" list is toxic or negative people. Be very careful whom you associate with. As you get older, you may grow in different directions from your old friends. Maybe you've learned to be dependent on certain people and got used to them being around. But sometimes you have to give up on the toxic relationships that could be draining you instead of serving you. I'm not saying you can't be friends with people. I'm just advising that you eliminate the negative influence they may have on your life. You may try to convince them because you love them but you don't want that influence constantly going into your mind so limit your time together.

I believe that most people start out with good intentions but, thanks to issues they've faced in business or in their personal life, they become negative, pessimistic people who are always playing devil's advocate and who are challenging or argumentative. These people believe that you must agree with their every opinion and that the world revolves around them. That type of person is always hoping that others fail, especially those like you who are trying to build something big. This mindset doesn't fit well into your business. We are all here for a purpose, with our own goals and dreams. We all have a mission or vision for life and as you build a team you want people who have similar dreams, goals and values so that you can enjoy harmony.

People will often choose team members because they want to make a lot of money but I would prefer a team member who's positive, excited and works hard versus a negative team member who is productive. You may disagree but I believe the environment and the culture that you maintain helps a team grow in the long run. Although you'd like to help everyone you must build a positive culture first. That culture won't always match the people you'd like to bring into your business and, although they might very well be productive, their attitude may not be a match for the rest of the team.

A team built primarily of negative people won't sustain. There will be jealousy and backstabbing. It's called the crab mentality—as one crab tries to get out of the bucket another crab pulls him down. It's almost guaranteed to happen with a negative culture. I hate to say it, but there are people who just want to argue, who just want to be right and who don't ever want to change, no matter how it disrupts the team. I can't stress this point too strongly: be very careful of toxic or negative people who are joining your business. They can and will hurt you.

Having said that, I'm a firm believer that you could be the light to help these people but be careful if it's influencing you in a negative way, to a point where it's taking away your joy and fulfillment because you're constantly battling the negative.

STOP WASTING TIME

Sometimes we need to take a short break from all the action and just relax. What I mean by wasting time is when you're doing nothing for an extended period of time. There's no urgency in your actions and you're living a very casual life. "Oh, whatever. I don't care what happens."

You are undoubtedly good at something and there are people out there who need help, leadership, training or maybe just an inspiring success story. If you don't use your talents, you could be denying others who could learn from you. Give yourself deadlines for what you want to achieve daily.

There's a difference between priority management and time management. In sales, your priority is prospecting but many sales people don't focus on that very well. Connecting with prospects is critical in the sales world but most people don't focus on priorities, they focus on time management. They drop off their dry cleaning, get coffee, wash their car and do a whole bunch of other chores but they fail to accomplish their priority for that day, which is to make calls and be productive.

Going to the gym to keep your body in shape is a priority, not a luxury. Reading for business knowledge and speaker training is a priority, not a luxury. You need to manage your time each day based on the priorities that your business deems necessary to be successful.

Be a Good Person

One thing that I can control is being a good person. One message my father and mother always conveyed is, "If you're going to do it, do it right." It's not an easy battle and I fail sometimes but the goal is to do what's right.

Honor your commitments, not only to yourself but also to others. Tell the truth, be honest with people and tell them what's on your mind. Sometimes that backfires on me because I'm a little bit over the top, but telling the truth is honesty. Don't say yes when you really mean no because you don't want to make someone feel bad. That's a tough one for some people to understand.

My favorite tip is to be humble no matter how great you might be. I remember times in my life when things were great and I lost my humility. It's amazing what happens to your ego when you reach success but you could also lose it quickly. Humility is one of the hardest things for people to maintain when they start doing well. I always try to remind myself that I'm not here because I'm anything special. I'm here because I was led to be this way. It was a gift that God gave me. You can fill in that blank however you want but for me it's God. I'm here because I was given a gift that I appreciate and that I'm humbled by. I know that what He gave me He could also take away. When you're humble, people will be more attracted to you.

Another tip is to look for the good in everyone. Depending on how you were brought up, you may not always see the good in people. I used to always look for the bad. But when you look for the bad that's exactly what you get in a team building business. Instead, limit that thought process and always look for the good in everyone. One key factor in team building that many people overlook is praise and recognition, two of the greatest motivators ever. I was taught that we should recognize even the smallest things. Recognize your children, recognize your wife. In business, recognize when new people come onboard, recognize that they're working hard to get their license or they're working hard to get their business started or they're working hard to go to meetings or they're working hard to be dedicated.

I love to give awards and small gifts because I appreciate what people have done. Most people work for many years and never get any kind of recognition. So as you build your team, make recognition a major part of your business. Help everyone get to where they want to go. Focus on recognizing more people and then watch your team grow because they see that you appreciate what they do. It's an amazing dynamic that many seem to overlook. They never recognize others because they crave the recognition so much for themselves. You know, we give out certificates or big trophies or plaques. I'm telling you, that goes a long way.

People won't believe in someone who's unsure of themselves. You've got to be solid in believing that people need your program, that people want to do business with you because you have great intentions, a great mindset and you want to build something big. You win in this business because they see that you're hungry, focused, and passionate and you truly care. In the team building business you win with your heart not with your head. Sometimes you have to get emotionally involved with your team or your leaders because you've got to care about people in order for them to trust you.

I've met many people who can recruit a team but they can't sustain it because they don't want to get emotionally involved. They don't want to get too close because they're worried that people will know too much about them. In team building, you can't just say I care with words. You have to truly care with your heart and really listen to people. Believe it or not, even your body language is important. In my opinion it's often more powerful than verbal language. That's one of the biggest secrets to building a team.

The RHINO mentality is understanding that fear can't stop you. Most people won't try anything new because they're afraid to fail. I've followed the philosophy that says, to overcome fear, do what you fear the most. Attack your fear; don't let it control you.

Attitude is everything. I believe you should always be positive, excited and enthusiastic. People love people who are excited. They don't like whiners or complainers or negative people. Nobody wants to be around a dull, frustrated, negative crybaby, so be positive. Be excited about life and be excited about being a RHINO!

Be a leader. Be a motivator. Be an honest, sincere leader. Be a builder who helps others get where they want to go. Be an example of a congruent life and be a winner. There's nothing wrong with wanting to be a winner, right? I like people with a RHINO mentality to lead a team. They help motivate others to win and to dream big.

Lastly, don't ask someone to do something that you wouldn't do. Make sure you lead by example and set high expectations. You'll develop an amazing winning team.

About Jeff Delgado

Jeffrey J. Delgado is a motivational speaker, trainer and 20-year financial services veteran who holds his Series 6 and 63 Life & Health Insurance Licenses. He leads a team of representatives in the San Francisco Bay Area and Southern California.

As the co-founder of Retiring America, Jeffrey has built a highly experienced team of financial professionals who are keenly focused on the fundamentals of building and preserving wealth.

Jeffrey lives in South San Francisco with his wife Emily and their two daughters, Shirley and Julia. His hobbies include working out, basketball and movies. He enjoys reading books to advance his knowledge and gain motivation. Those close to Jeffrey describe him as genuine, influential, ambitious, positive, passionate and straightforward. His rigorous work ethic and optimistic attitude combined with his strong spiritual faith contribute to his success. Jeffrey's motto for success is: "Whoever is happiest wins!"

Chavez Media

Rick Chavez enjoyed a successful career as a Bay Area TV/Radio anchor and voiceover talent, interviewing Hall of Fame athletes, Olympic champions and Silicon Valley executives. He was Sports Director at NBC11 in San Jose and anchored at ABC7 and KRON4 in San Francisco. Rick hosted Cisco's first international SMB webcast from The Netherlands. In addition, he anchored Oracle webcasts in New Orleans and San Diego. Rick produced

Silicon Valley tech reports for CNBC-Europe, was the host of *"Best of the Bay"* and won four Telly Awards for broadcast and documentary production excellence.

Rick was Jubilee Bible College Valedictorian in 2011 and now specializes in authoring books for a variety of audiences. He is available to work with other authors as a freelance editor, proofreader or publisher. Please contact chavezmedia@gmail.com.

73337713R00048

Made in the USA
Columbia, SC
09 September 2019